YOUR KNOWLEDGE HAS VALUE

AF143970

- We will publish your bachelor's and master's thesis, essays and papers

- Your own eBook and book - sold worldwide in all relevant shops

- Earn money with each sale

Upload your text at www.GRIN.com
and publish for free

Bibliographic information published by the German National Library:

The German National Library lists this publication in the National Bibliography; detailed bibliographic data are available on the Internet at http://dnb.dnb.de .

Imprint:

Copyright © 2007 GRIN Verlag, Open Publishing GmbH
Print and binding: Books on Demand GmbH, Norderstedt Germany
ISBN: 9783638944991

This book at GRIN:

http://www.grin.com/en/e-book/90976/making-history-and-making-it-over

Stefan Zeidler

Making History and Making it Over

The Role of Metafiction for the Understanding of History

GRIN Publishing

GRIN - Your knowledge has value

Since its foundation in 1998, GRIN has specialized in publishing academic texts by students, college teachers and other academics as e-book and printed book. The website www.grin.com is an ideal platform for presenting term papers, final papers, scientific essays, dissertations and specialist books.

Visit us on the internet:

http://www.grin.com/

http://www.facebook.com/grincom

http://www.twitter.com/grin_com

Making History and Making it Over

The Role of Metafiction for the Understanding of History

25.09.2007

Stefan Zeidler

Freie Universität Berlin
Institut für Englische Philologie
Surveying English Literatures II: Historical Novels through
Time
Sommersemester 2007

Contents

Introduction

Our time – this refers to the major part of our population - of demystified heroes and legends, has only a vague understanding of history and struggles for its interpretation.

History in this context does not only mean the mere sequence of specific incidents and events that cannot be changed retroactively by any access to the past. This concept is furthermore a discussion on these events that is their interpretation. That means that history is and in this form it is most likely to be perceived, the connection of object and subject, referring to the events in the temporal past and its spectator in the present. This creates a subjective ribbon that connects temporal past and present by dint of an interpretive frame. Indeed the past cannot be changed, but its interpretation and analysis can be.

This is exactly the approach of Stephen Fry who provides with his novel *Making History* a possible answer to the question, how Germany and the world might have developed without Adolf Hitler. Supported by historical facts and enriched by fictitious elements, Fry's novel affords the reader a manual for the exposure to one's own past and distorts the understanding of history of the broad majority who ascertains a single man, Adolf Hitler, to be the root for all evil.

The following text tries to analyze the role of historical fiction for one's accomplishment of history in general and how Fry in particular does away with the common view that history is barely more than the sequence of big men's big actions.

Therefore, I would like to proceed from the assumption that *Making History* is a critical metaphor for the work of historiographs who create history by interpreting, omitting and stressing of historical facts. The novel also expresses one's responsibility for the past one builds his present and future on. Fry uses his protagonist's thesis, the "Meisterwerk" as a metafictional element to clarify the meaning of historical fiction for developing the understanding of history. Furthermore I will try to clarify the novel's affiliation to the genre of metahistoriography after a short theoretical digression about this literary field.

The Concept of History and Fry's Interpretation of History

Usually the term history means all that was and happened in the past. It refers to something completed that cannot be changed due to access from the present. It is also "unrepeatable" – at least in a strict sense. In the case of *Making History* this logical approach does not work anymore. In his novel, Fry does change the historical plot from the 1st june of 1888 and thus converges to the postmodernism's discourse on historiography and reality. It raises the question, whether historiography has to be regarded as fiction. Lionel Gossman offers a good account of Fry's assumed writing intentions: "Modern history and modern literature [...] have both rejected the ideal of representation [...]. Both now conceive of their work as exploration, testing, creation of new meanings, rather than disclosure or revelation of meanings already in some sense 'there'" (Hutcheon 15f).

So Fry's novel is not about victims of the Nazi terror and how they cope with their past. It is about historiography in general and the thin ridge a historian walks on while analyzing and interpreting past events. Although the past cannot be changed – the author will stick to the differentiation between the term past as the events and the term history as their textualised interpretation – their interpretation can be. Postmodernism has assumed that history only exists due to textuality and must hence be regarded as fiction, too. Postmodern writer Linda Hutcheon, Professor of English and Comparative Literature at the University of Toronto, expressed this as follows:

> "History is not made obsolete: it is, however, being rethought – as a human construct. And in arguing that history does not exist except as text, it does not [...] deny that the past existed, but only that its accessibility to us now is entirely conditioned by textuality. We cannot know the past except through its texts" (Hutcheon 16).

This concept of textuality refers not only to written texts but to a society's collective and cultural memory including the spoken word and traditional narrations since history is not sensible directly. The following digression intends to give a short overview of metafiction and especially of Linda Hutcheon's concept of metahistoriography as a help to identify Fry's novel as metafictional.

Short Digression on Metafiction

The term metafiction refers to a self-critical, usually extra-textual reference that on the one hand keeps the reader aware of the text's fictive character and on the other hand criticizes the genre itself. Sir Walter Scott's *Waverley Novels* function as a landmark of metafictional writing about a historical topic. Scott's narrator speaks directly to the reader and reflects on the process of finding a proper name for the protagonist and on the readers' habits concerning historic novels. Although in comparably humble extent and frequency only, these metafictional, extratextual utterances keep the reader aware of the representation's artificial character (Bölling 31f).

In the period of postmodernism, historiography and the construct of history in general were problematized and selfreferential elements were functionalized to accomplish this purpose. The main critique of historiography was and still is that an incident as such does not have a meaning by itself. It is applied retrospectively by historians who choose single events from the temporal continuum and bring them in a meaningful order. Although questioning the epistemological status of historical 'fact' and the distrust of apparent neutrality and objectivity were not an invention of postmodernism, they were mainly problematized in that period (Bölling 39). Postmodernism stressed the nature of history as a matter of knowledge of the past one has in the present and raised the question how that past can be known and what can be known of it. This created the main criteria of metafictional texts: the functionalized contradiction between the stress on the representation's fictive character on the one hand and on the extratextual referent's reality on the other.

Linda Hutcheon defines historiographic metafiction as a variety of metafiction that "incorporates all three areas of concern [fiction, history, theory]" (Bölling 41) and added that metafiction is alike history itself a construct to understand the past. Hutcheon's strict definition of historiographic metafiction as equivalent to postmodernism was later criticized and led to further development of her theory. Kurt Müller regards historiographic metafiction as an outstanding genre in contemporary American literature and refers to the various representations of American history from social minorities' points of view revising the common sense image of history (Müller 50). He distinguishes between two "apparently opposed modes of metahistoriographic de-construction and re-construction" (Müller 48) providing the two poles of a scale and allow a more precise allocation. Texts of the first group present a history differing from the common sense history image as real, whereas texts of the second group not only present a different history but stress their fictive status. Between these two poles range all possible kinds of historiographic metafiction that were not necessarily conceived in postmodernism. Another distinction is made by Ansgar Nünning between implicit and explicit forms of metafiction. While the explicit version uses a fictional narrator to broach historiotheoretical issues, implicit metafiction cannot be isolated as discrete passages but is accessible only in the thematic and structural context of the entire novel (Nünning 297-343). Following his definition, historiographic metafiction should be called fictional metahistoriography since it uses the means of fiction to examine metahistorical issues (Nünning 284).

Michael Young and his "Meisterwerk" as Metafictional References

Although Fry's novel lacks the extratextual instance that in the previous chapter was mentioned as a characteristic of metafictional texts, it deals nevertheless critically with the past time event's analysis by his protagonist's doctoral thesis, the so called "Meisterwerk". Hence *Making History* has to be regarded as implicit metahistoriographic fiction.

Michael Young, graduate in history is not only the novel's protagonist but the projection screen for metahistoriographic issues. His rejected thesis not only tells the story of the young Adolf Hitler in extracts as a story parallel to the actual storyline, but thematizes exemplarily the "making" of history. Classifying popular historians at the beginning of the novel as either belonging stylistically to the forties and fifties on the one hand or the sixties and seventies on the other, Young comes to the conclusion that both, the fogeyish and heavy historian are outdated and that a historian should belong to his own past more than anyone else to understand what happened in the past (Fry 63). This assumption refers to the discourse concerning the retrospective generation of sense of certain events in the past, a process that Young defines as to "historifying" the past (Fry 63). In a conversation with Leo Zuckerman, Young states that historians from the forties and fifties had the advantage of being able to talk to victims and witnesses of the Holocaust, granting them direct access to the past whereas he as a "history surfer" (Fry 64) can only examine old notes, recordings and other historians' interpretations of the past. He resumes that he did not come across anything that had not been seen before and refers again to the historiography's issue of direct access to the past.

When his supervisor Fraser-Stuart refuses the thesis by reason of its fictitious elements, he refers to it not as an academic argument but as a novel. This also has to be regarded as an implicit instance of metahistoriography since it describes a historian's work as filling up historical gaps between certain incidents to apply a meaning retrospectively. Young does not

25. September 2007

have any proofs and attributions for the unorthodox "linking passages" (Fry 91) that only serve the purpose to make it a more readable by adding color and drama. The reader now understands the nature of the seemingly asserted chapters about Klara, giving birth to Adolf and her brutish husband Alois as the literal historical fiction about the early years of Adolf Hitler and the later rise of Rudolf Gloder. Fry's change of writing style to that of a film script in the chapter "Making Movies" and its application on later chapters, does not only raise the tension but also keeps the reader constantly aware of the story's fictitious character. Another explicit instance of metafictionality can be found, when the narrator reminds the reader of the circular nature of the story that complicates its access. His statement that "A: None of what follows ever happened" and "B: All of what followed is entirely true" (Fry 238) and the reference to a good historian's abilities once again stress the novel's metafictional character and demand the reader to think about the given representation of reality as construct.

The alternative history, caused by Young's and Zuckerman's attempt to change the past by circumvention of a single person's, namely Adolf Hitler's, birth parallels the present representation of reality and therewith illustrates the connection between the temporal past and the present. By this attempt and its consequences, Fry makes clear that history is just a construction whose meaning exists between single incidents and can be changed by their omission or emphasis.

Metahistoriography and Cultural Memory - Outlook

Although we know that the past cannot be changed by access from the present, Fry's novel *Making History* shows impressively that even if certain events **could** be changed, the consequences would be unpredictable. History is not a logical sequence of big men's big actions but a complex construct, a fact clarified by the rise of Rudolf Gloder instead of the unborn Adolf Hitler. His exclusive guilt for the Holocaust and the inhuman cruelties under his cabinet were as well constructed by a zeitgeist that could not accept and understand a whole nation's guilt as Fry's world without Hitler. Public consciousness tends to forget that Anti-Semitism and National Socialist ideas already existed before Hitler as well as the economy crisis, the lack of democratic tradition, race ideologies and the humiliation by the Allies existed independently from his person.

The question "What if?" will always be unanswered but metahistoriographic texts introduce the reader to the issue of historiography and invite him to get an idea of the past, that is to own his past, the basic requirement for shaping the future consciously. Since commemoration

25. September 2007

and critical discourse are not sole state affairs but need to be lived by people, metahistoriographic novels are part of the communicative memory that legitimates and criticizes the support of a particular present. In playing an important role in forgetting as well as in understanding what WAS and also what IS, the collective memory helps people to allocate in time. In George Orwell's novel *1984*, the ruling party controlled the cultural memory making it impossible for the people to allocate themselves and thus to go into critical distance.

Cultural memory allows for our living in two parallel times, the past and the present, but it demands a constant maintenance, a fact that makes a society's cultural memory easy to manipulate. This maintenance is provided inter alia by literature and historical fiction in particular. That is why in the recent book about a young magician's adventures, the protagonist has to face folkish race ideologies whose fictitious propagator's race delusion has been compared with real Adolf Hitler's. People stumble over time's fragments and it is the novelist's task to make this a smooth and easy to follow, guiding path by inviting the reader to look into the subject of his own past and to derive historical consciousness out of it.

List of Works Cited

Bölling, Gordon. History in the Making. Heidelberg: Unterversitätsverlag Winter, 2006.

Fry, Stephen. Making History. London: Arrow Books, 2004.

Hutcheon, Linda. A Poetics of Postmodernism. History, Theory, Fiction. London: Routledge, 1988.

Müller, Kurt. "The Development Toward Historiographic Metafiction in the American Novel." Bernd Engler, and Kurt Müller (eds.). Historiographic Metafiction in Modern American and Canadian Literature: Beiträge zur englischen und amerikanischen Literatur. Paderborn: Schöningh, 1994. 35-51.

Nünning, Ansgar. Von historischer Fiktion zu historiographischer Metafiktion, Band 1: LIR Litatur, Imagination, Realität. Trier: WVT Wissenschaftlicher Verlag Trier, 1995.

25. September 2007

YOUR KNOWLEDGE HAS VALUE

- We will publish your bachelor's and
  master's thesis, essays and papers

- Your own eBook and book -
  sold worldwide in all relevant shops

- Earn money with each sale

Upload your text at www.GRIN.com
and publish for free